To: Grandma

From:

Dear Grandma,

I want you to know you are a *Queen*, and without you I would not be the person I am today. You are a special and irreplaceable part of our family, that continues to bestow your wisdom, encouragement and guidance. You are my confidant, my bestfriend and guardian angel here on Earth. While I may not tell you this enough, I love and appreciate everything you do for me. I have personalized this book for you to express my gratitude. Thank you for being a part of my life, and my Grandma!

Love always,

-xoxo

This Is Why I Love You...

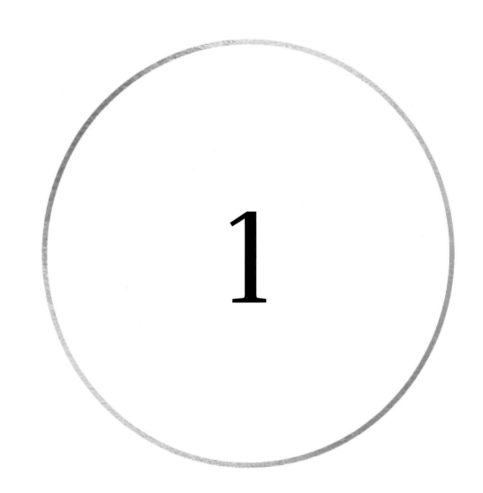

1

Thank You For Teaching Me

_____

_____

_____

_____

_____

_____

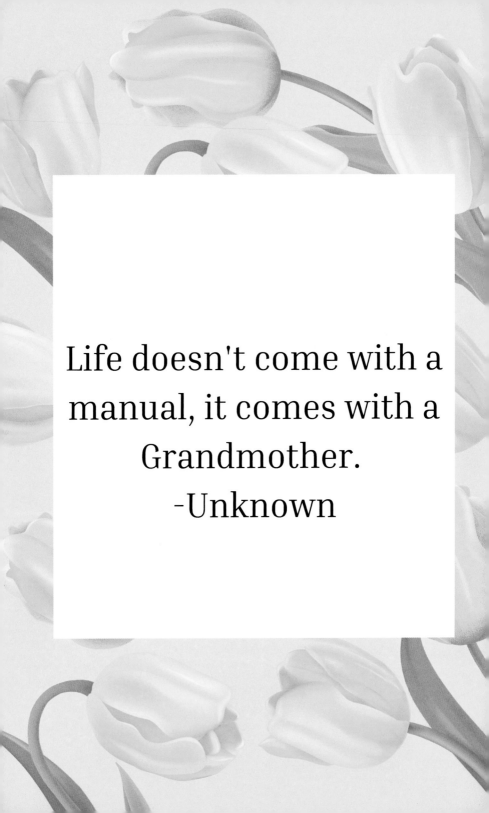

Life doesn't come with a manual, it comes with a Grandmother.
-Unknown

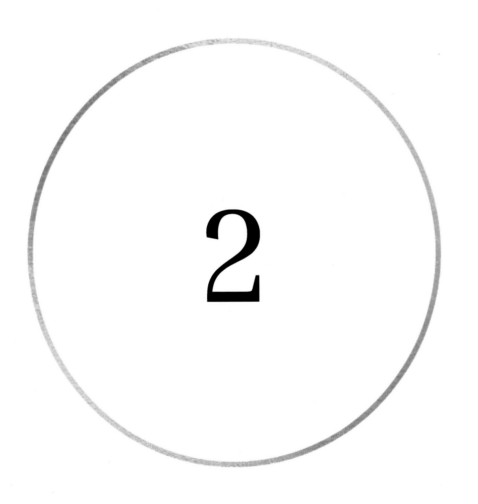

I Love That You're My Grandma Because

_____

_____

_____

_____

_____

_____

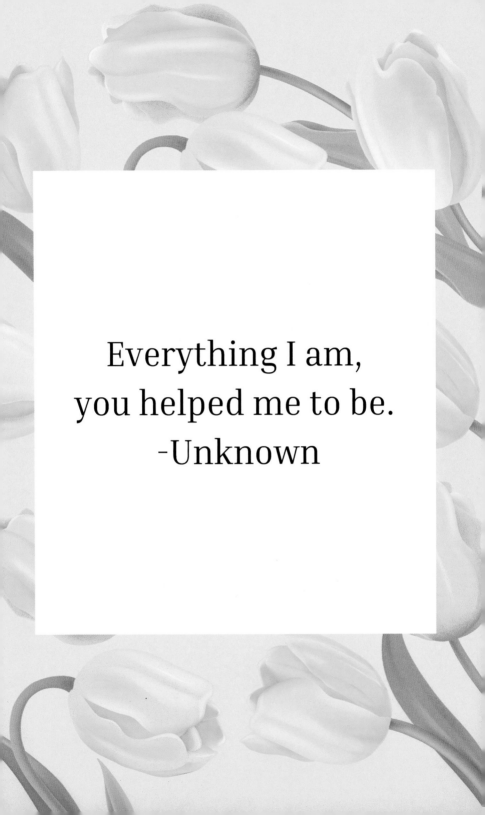

Everything I am,
you helped me to be.
-Unknown

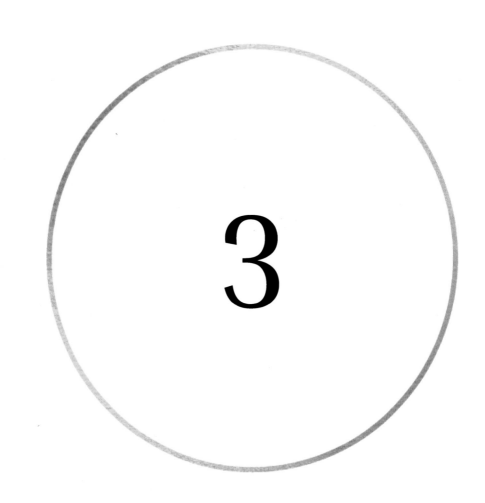

3

You Inspire Me To

_____

_____

_____

_____

_____

_____

Grandmas are short on criticism and long on love.
-Unknown

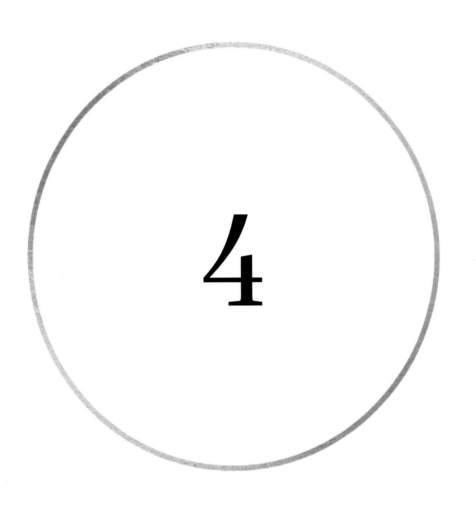

4

My Favorite Memory Of Us

_____

_____

_____

_____

_____

_____

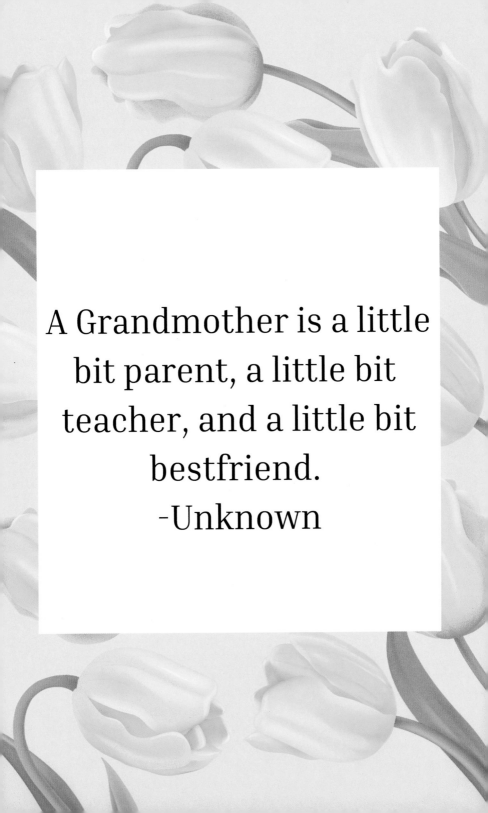

A Grandmother is a little bit parent, a little bit teacher, and a little bit bestfriend.
-Unknown

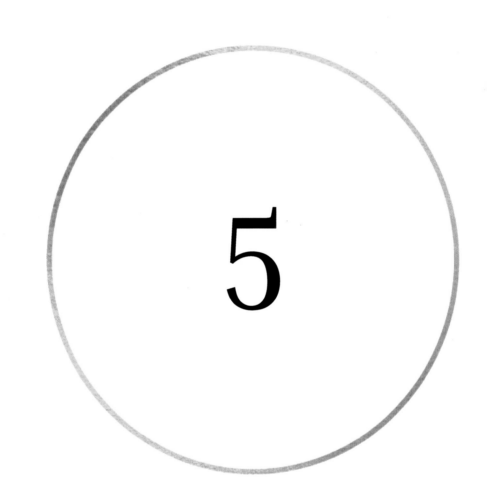

5

The Best Thing About You Is

_____

_____

_____

_____

_____

_____

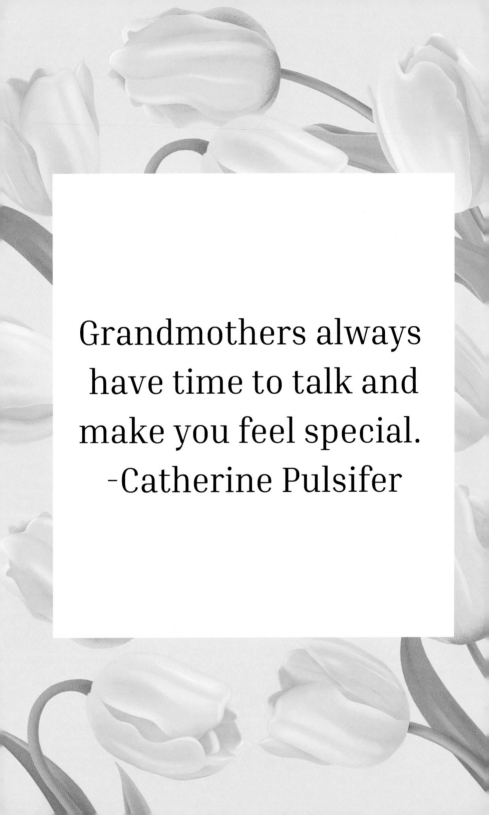

Grandmothers always have time to talk and make you feel special.
-Catherine Pulsifer

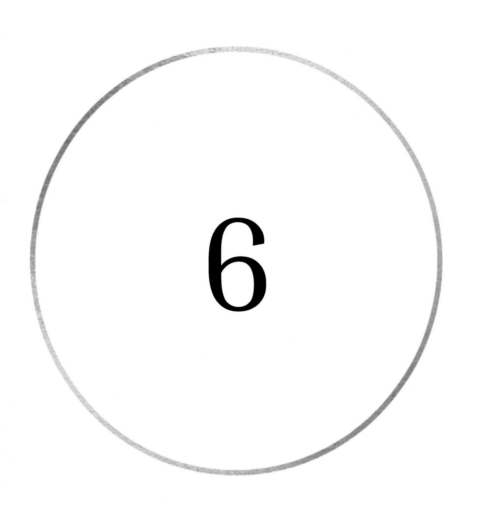

I Always Smile When You

_____

_____

_____

_____

_____

_____

If nothing is going well,
call your Grandmother.
-Italian Proverb

You Always Made Me Feel

_____

_____

_____

_____

_____

_____

My Grandmother is my angel on earth.
-Catherine Pulsifer

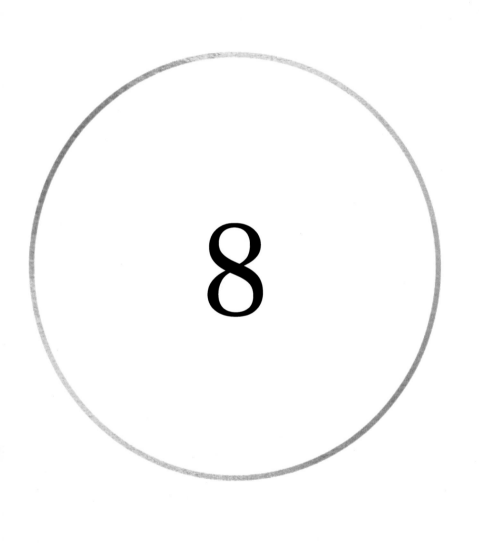

8

You Taught Me

_____

_____

_____

_____

_____

_____

There's no place like home except Grandma's.
-Unknown

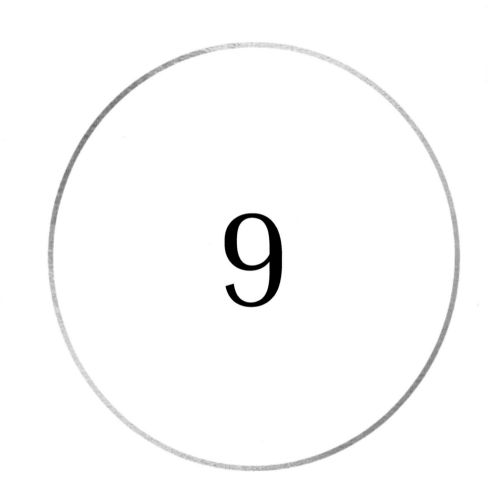

9

I Love It When You Call Me

_____

_____

_____

_____

_____

_____

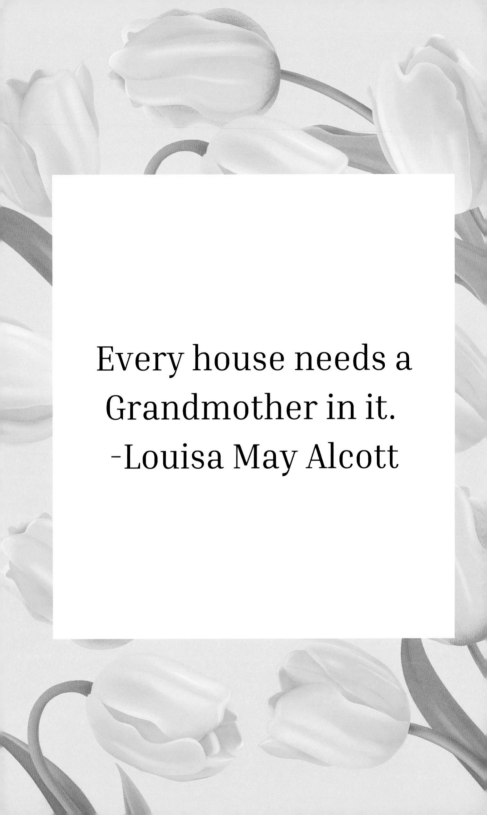

Every house needs a
Grandmother in it.
-Louisa May Alcott

10

You Are Good At

_____

_____

_____

_____

_____

_____

A garden of love grows in a Grandmother's heart.
-Unknown

11

If You Were A Dessert You Would Be

_____

_____

_____

_____

_____

_____

Grandmothers and roses
are much the same. Each
is God's masterpiece
with different names.
-Unknown

12

These Words Make Me Think Of You

_____

_____

_____

_____

_____

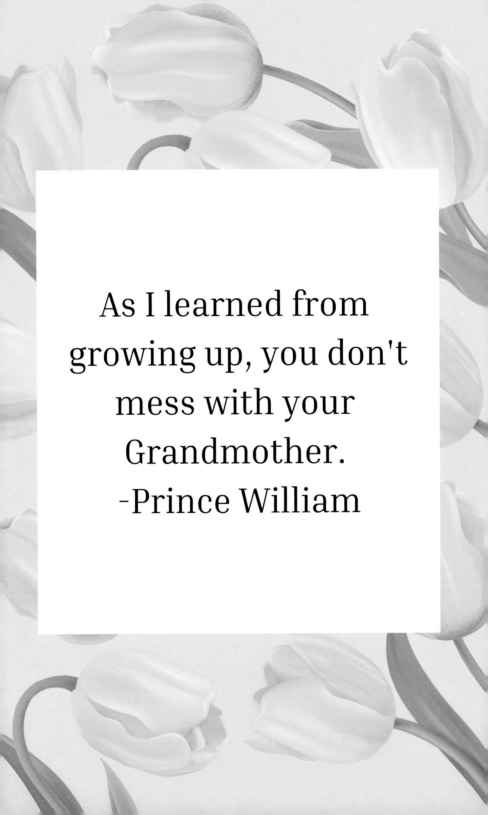

As I learned from growing up, you don't mess with your Grandmother.
-Prince William

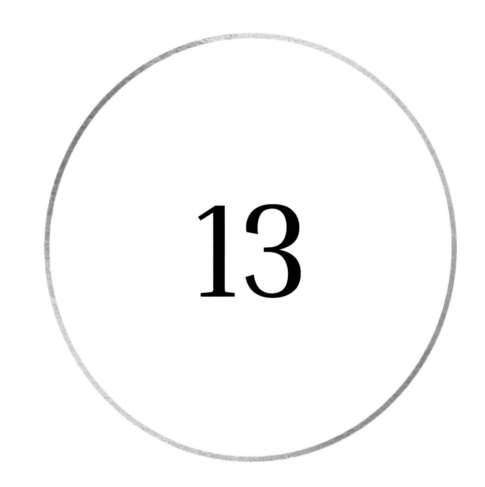

13

If You Had A Superpower It Would Be

Every parent knows that children look at their Grandparents as sources of wisdom and security.
-David Jeremiah

14

I Love When We

_____

_____

_____

_____

_____

_____

Grandmas never run out of hugs or cookies.

-Unknown

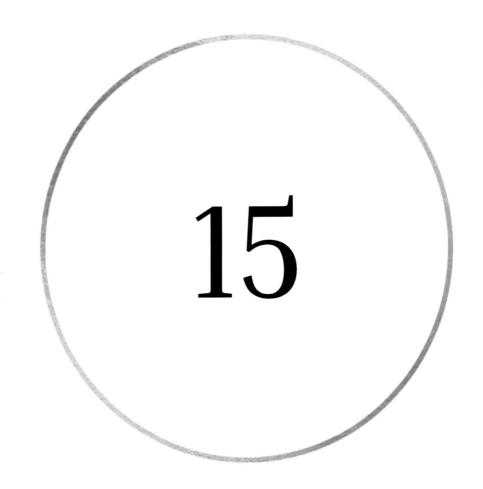

15

The Funniest Thing You Do Is

_____

_____

_____

_____

_____

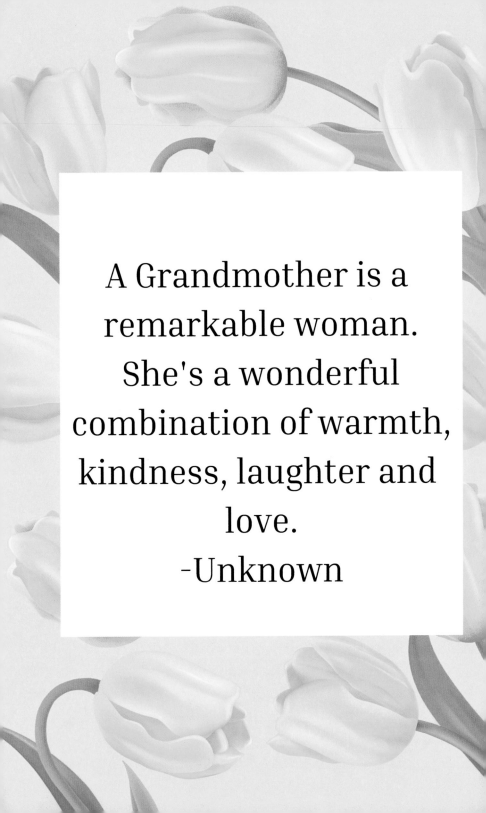

A Grandmother is a remarkable woman. She's a wonderful combination of warmth, kindness, laughter and love.
-Unknown

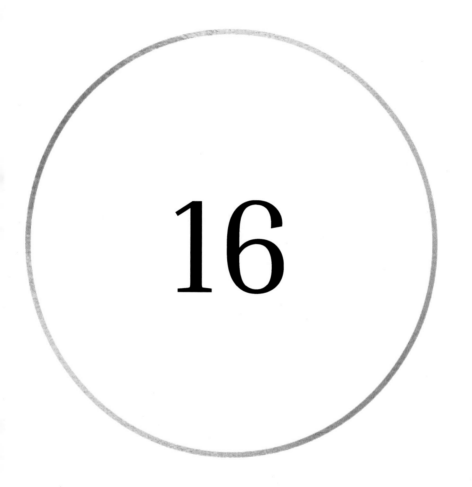

16

I Love Remembering The Time We Went To

_____

_____

_____

_____

_____

_____

A Grandma is warm hugs and sweet memories. She remembers all of your accomplishments and forgets all of your mistakes.
-Barbara Cage

17

I Love
Getting Advice On

_____

_____

_____

_____

_____

_____

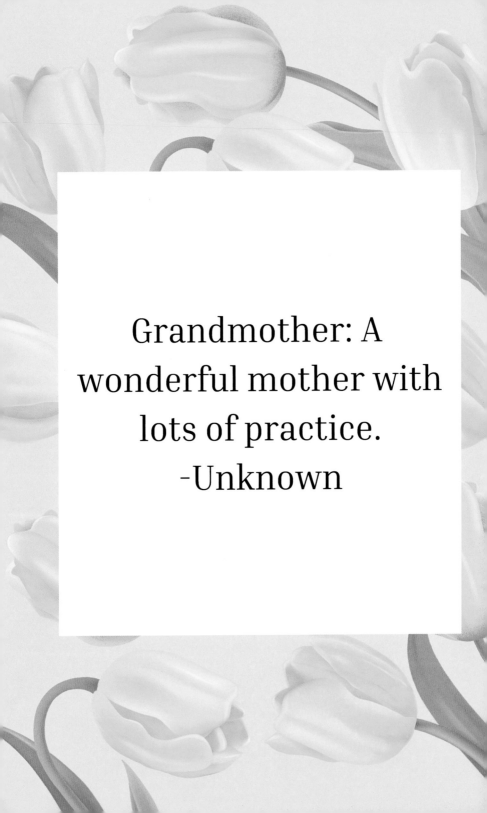

Grandmother: A wonderful mother with lots of practice.
-Unknown

18

I Know You Love Me Because

_____

_____

_____

_____

_____

_____

Grandmothers are voices of the past and role models of the present. Grandmothers open the doors to the future.
-Helen Ketchum

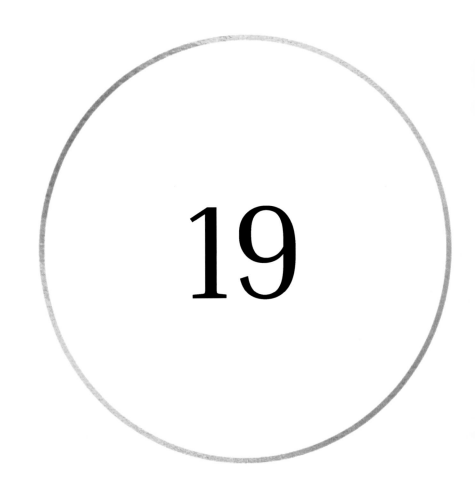

19

You Were There
For Me When

_____

_____

_____

_____

_____

_____

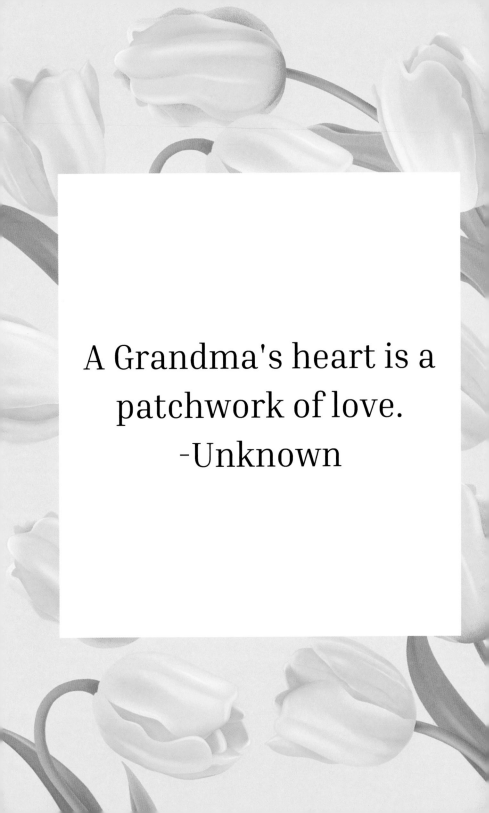

A Grandma's heart is a patchwork of love. -Unknown

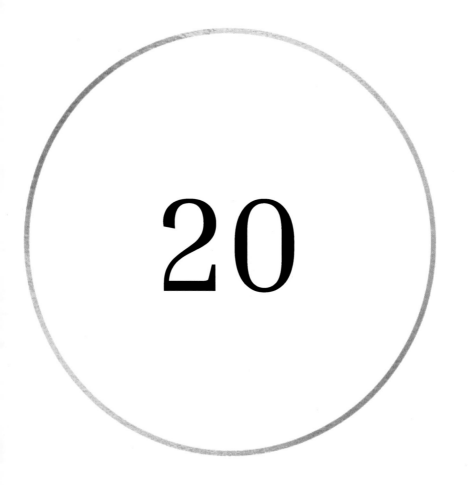
20

My Funniest Memory Of Us

_____

_____

_____

_____

_____

_____

A Grandmother is both
a sword and a shield.
-Fredrik Backman

21

I Love It When We Play

_____

_____

_____

_____

_____

_____

_____

When a child is born, so are Grandmothers.
-Judith Levy

22

If You Were A Scent You Would Be

_____

_____

_____

_____

_____

_____

Grandmothers open up
a new world of change,
challenge, and
celebration in a
woman's life.
-Rebecca B. Jordan

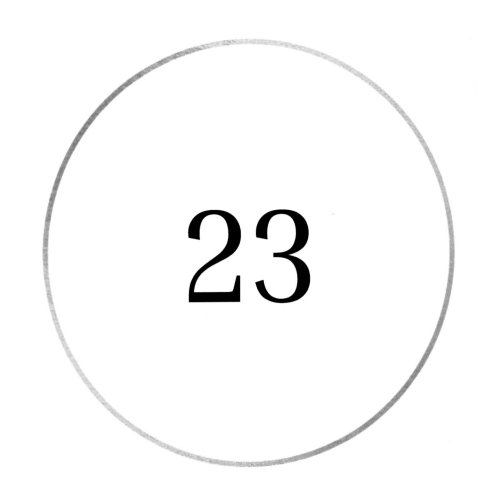

23

The World Needs To Know About Your

_____

_____

_____

_____

_____

_____

Grandmas are moms
with lots of frosting.
-Unknown

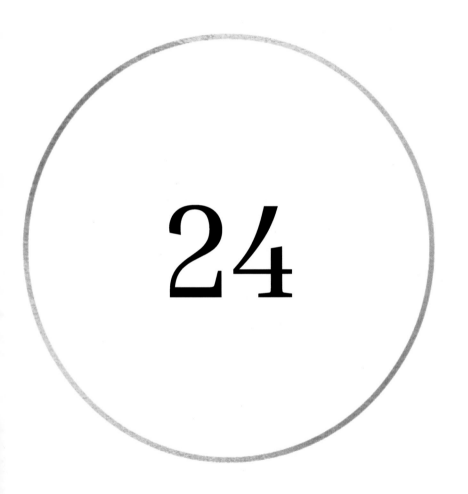

24

I Love The Sound Of Your

_____

_____

_____

_____

_____

_____

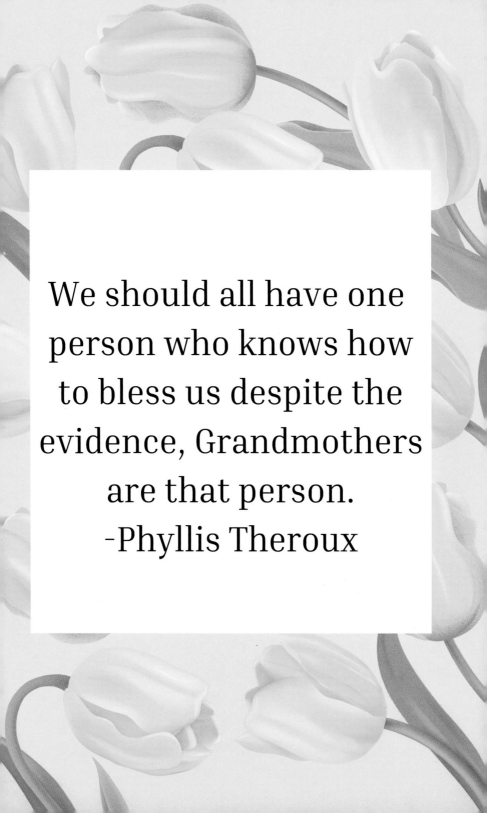

We should all have one person who knows how to bless us despite the evidence, Grandmothers are that person.
-Phyllis Theroux

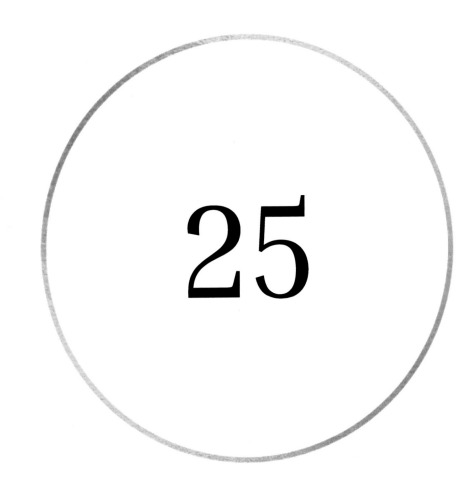

25

I'm Happy You Showed Me How To

_____

_____

_____

_____

_____

_____

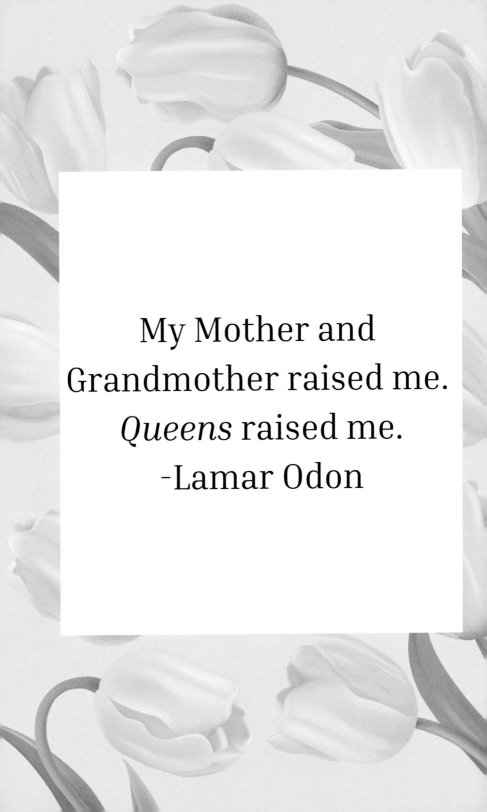

My Mother and Grandmother raised me. *Queens* raised me.
-Lamar Odon

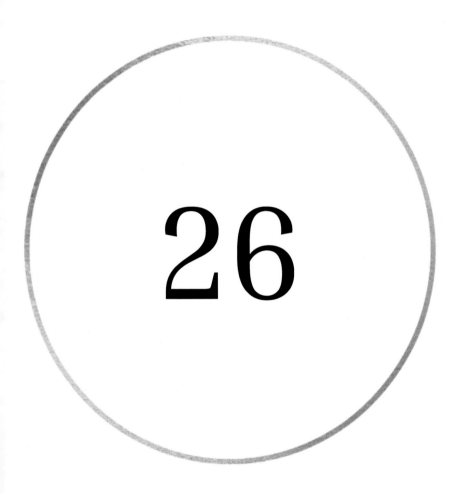

26

If I Had To Describe You In One Word

_____

_____

_____

_____

_____

_____

Grandmothers are a gift
not to be taken lightly.
So many lose them,
before they are old
enough to know their
magic.
-Nikita Gill

27

You Made Me Laugh When

_____

_____

_____

_____

_____

_____

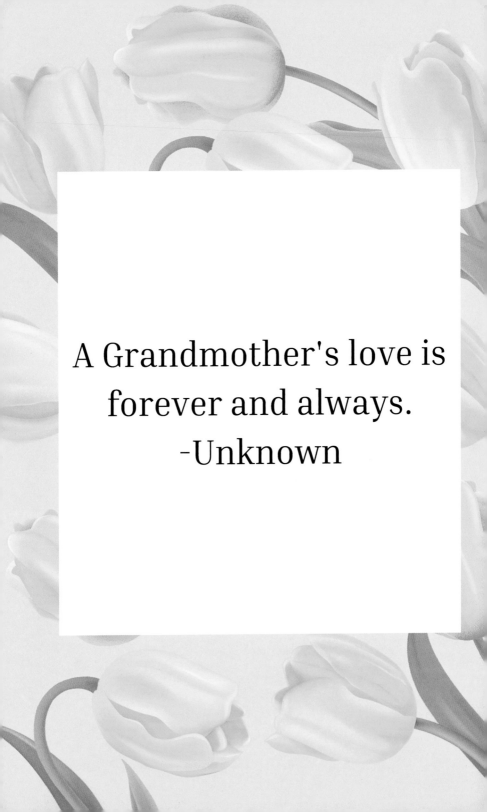

A Grandmother's love is forever and always.
-Unknown

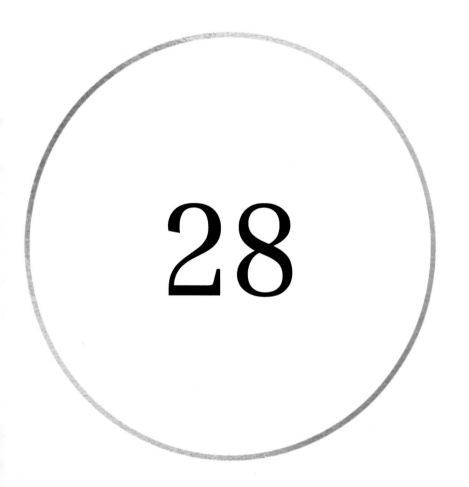

28

If You Were A Song You'd Be

_____

_____

_____

_____

_____

_____

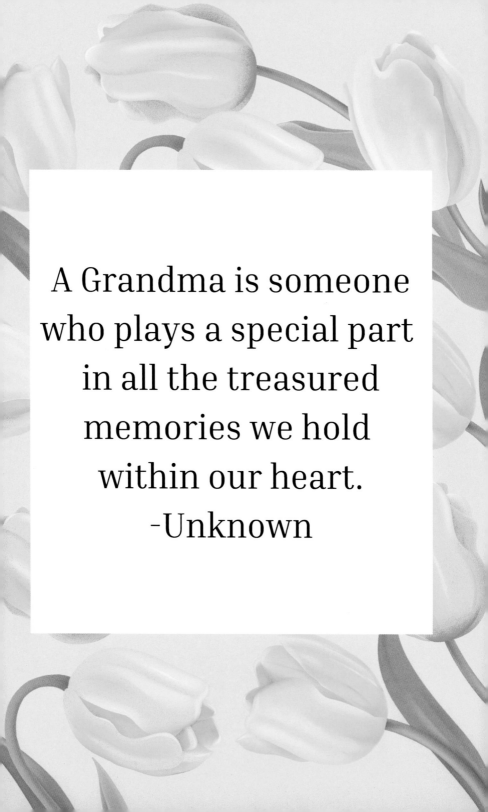

A Grandma is someone who plays a special part in all the treasured memories we hold within our heart.
-Unknown

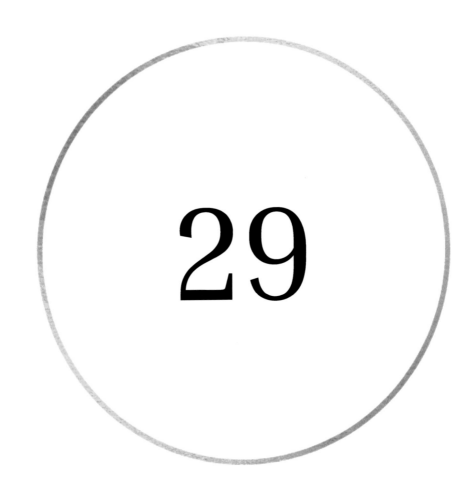

29

Thank You For

_____

_____

_____

_____

_____

_____

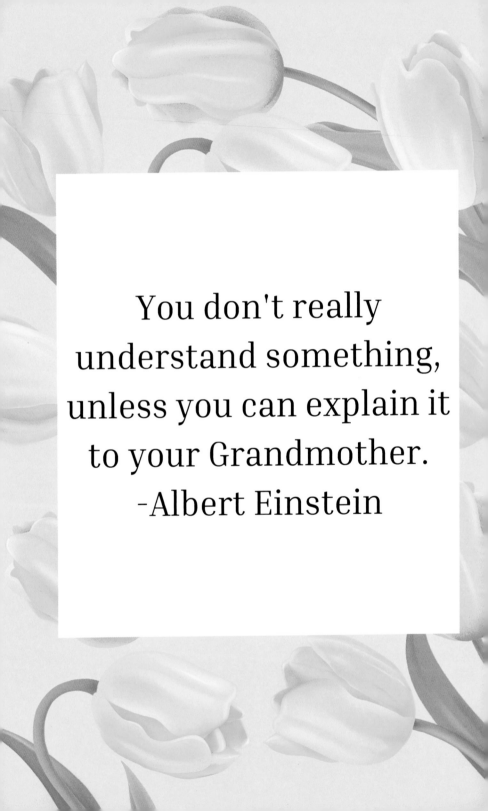

You don't really understand something, unless you can explain it to your Grandmother.
-Albert Einstein

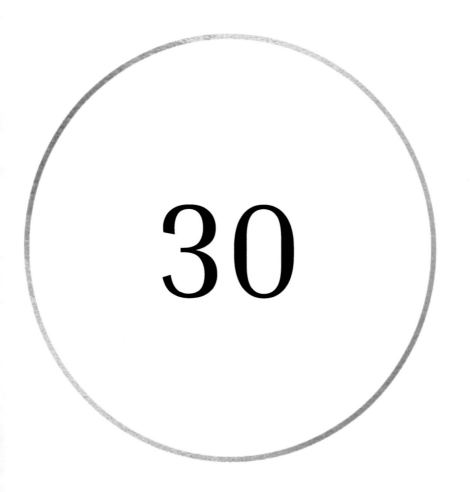

30

I Love How You Always Say

_____

_____

_____

_____

_____

A Grandma is someone who's dear in every way. Her smile is like the sunshine that brightens each new day.
-Unknown

Made in the USA
Monee, IL
02 May 2022

95727143R00057